P9-DLZ-390

INSECTS & SPIDERS

POISONOUS SPIDERS

Per Christiansen

Gareth Stevens
Publishing

Please visit our web site at www.garethstevens.com
For a free color catalog describing Gareth Stevens Publishing's
list of high-quality books, call 1-800-542-2595 (USA)
or 1-800-387-3178 (Canada).
Gareth Stevens Publishing's fax: 1-877-542-2596

Library of Congress Cataloging-in-Publication Data
available upon request from publisher.

ISBN-10: 0-8368-9219-4 (lib. bdg.)
ISBN-13: 978-0-8368-9219-2 (lib. bdg.)

This North American edition first published in 2009 by
Gareth Stevens Publishing
A Weekly Reader® Company
1 Reader's Digest Road
Pleasantville, NY 10570-7000 USA

7/10

Copyright © 2009 by Amber Books, Ltd.
Produced by Amber Books Ltd., Bradley's Close
74–77 White Lion Street
London N1 9PF, U.K.

Illustrations © International Masters Publishers AB

Project Editor: James Bennett
Design: Tony Cohen

Gareth Stevens Senior Managing Editor: Lisa M. Herrington
Gareth Stevens Editor: Joann Jovinelly
Gareth Stevens Creative Director: Lisa Donovan
Gareth Stevens Designer: Paul Bodley

Printed in the United States of America

1 2 3 4 5 6 7 8 9 10 09 08

Contents

Continents of the World

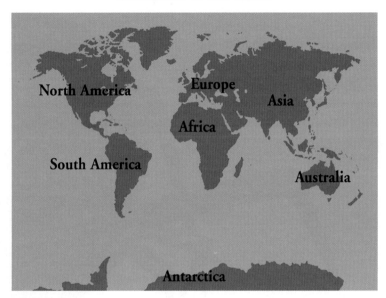

The world is divided into seven continents —
North America, South America, Europe, Africa,
Asia, Australia, and Antarctica. In this book,
the area where each animal lives is shown in red,
while all land is shown in green.

Words that appear in the glossary are printed in
boldface type the first time they occur in the text.

Australian Redback Spider

The female redback spider has a large, round **abdomen**. Inside its abdomen are hundreds of eggs. Male redback spiders are half the size of females and are much thinner.

The Australian redback spider is glossy black. A wide, red or orange stripe runs along its back.

Redback spider **mouthparts** are small and delicate. It is not the size of its **fangs** that make the redback so dangerous, but its **venom**.

Redback spiders have long, legs that contain thousands of tiny slits. These slits sense movement and **vibration**.

The Australian redback spider likes to set up its home near humans. It lives outdoors in woodpiles and buckets and in the eaves and gutters of houses.

1 A female redback spider rarely leaves the safety of her web. Males, however, wander around in search of females.

2 After **mating** with the larger female, the male cannot escape. The female's urge to feed is too strong.

3 The female bites the male and **injects** him with venom, which kills him immediately. She then eats him.

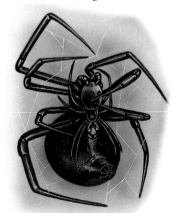

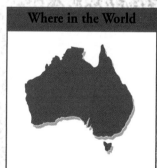

Black Widow Spider

Triangular red markings on the black widow's abdomen form an hourglass shape.

The black widow spider's legs end in tiny claws. It uses these for gripping its web and grabbing its **prey**.

The male black widow spider taps a special code on the female's web with its legs to avoid being eaten.

The black widow's eyes are arranged into two rows. Although it has eight eyes, its vision is poor.

The black widow spider gets its name because the female will sometimes kill and eat the much smaller male after mating.

1 The black widow spider chooses an area with a lot of twigs so it can weave its web between them. It then ejects a fluid from its abdomen that hardens in the air and becomes silk.

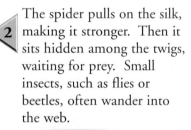

2 The spider pulls on the silk, making it stronger. Then it sits hidden among the twigs, waiting for prey. Small insects, such as flies or beetles, often wander into the web.

3 When a fly lands on the web, it sends vibrations through it. The spider senses these movements. It then kills the fly with a poisonous bite.

Actual Size

Did You Know?

The black widow is one of the most feared spiders in the world. It is highly **venomous** and has even been known to kill people. The spider bites people only to defend itself.

Where in the World

Black widows live in the United States, Mexico, and Central America.

Brazilian Wandering Spider

A spider's **pedipalps** are sense **organs**. They are covered with fine hairs that help locate prey.

The Brazillian wandering spider has long, strong legs. It does not rest in a web. Instead, the Brazilian wandering spider searches for its prey in places like log piles and fruit crates.

The Brazilian wandering spider has a pair of strong mouthparts. It bites and injects a deadly venom into its prey.

The reddish-brown Brazilian wandering spider is unrelated to tarantulas, even though it has a hairy body.

The Brazilian wandering spider's body can grow up to 1 inch (2.5 centimeters) long. The distance from the tip of one leg to the tip of its opposite leg can be 4 to 5 inches (10 to 13 cm).

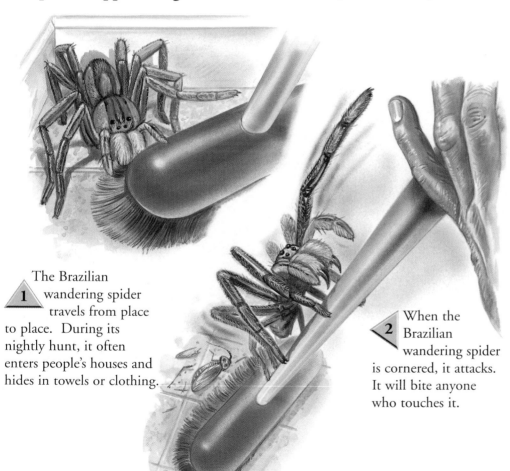

1. The Brazilian wandering spider travels from place to place. During its nightly hunt, it often enters people's houses and hides in towels or clothing.

2. When the Brazilian wandering spider is cornered, it attacks. It will bite anyone who touches it.

Size

Did You Know?

The Brazilian wandering spider is one of the most dangerous spiders in the world. It is **aggressive**, with a poisonous venom. Brazilian wandering spiders sometimes enter foreign countries in food containers.

Where in the World

The Brazilian wandering spider lives in South and Central America.

Hunting Spider

A hunting spider has a round abdomen. At the end of its abdomen are **silk glands**, known as **spinnerets**. But hunting spiders do not spin webs. They use their silk to make **cocoons** to protect their eggs.

The hunting spider's legs are long and sturdy. It is a fast-moving **predator**.

The hunting spider's jaws are so strong that it can lift its prey off a surface while pumping it full of venom.

The hairs on the hunting spider's legs help it locate its prey.

The hunting spider is one of the giants of the spider world. Its leg **span** can reach 5 to 6 inches (13 to 15 cm). A fierce killer, the hunting spider grabs its prey too quickly to be seen with the naked eye.

1 The hunting spider feeds on large insects, such as crickets and grasshoppers. It is powerful enough to attack small frogs, such as this tree frog.

2 The spider kills the frog with a venomous bite. The spider's venom is so **toxic** that a tree frog can be **paralyzed** in seconds.

Size

Did You Know?

Hunting spiders do not build webs, but wander around nightly in search of prey. They often enter people's houses through open windows. Most people welcome hunting spiders because they hunt cockroaches and other household pests.

Where in the World

The hunting spider lives in Central and South America.

Indian Ornamental Tarantula

The tarantula's legs are covered in hair. Some hairs are thinner than others. The thinnest hairs pick up vibrations in the air that reveal where prey is hiding.

The tarantula's head is lined with eight tiny eyes, but its eyesight is poor.

Like all spiders, tarantulas have a tough outer skeleton called an **exoskeleton**. As tarantulas grow, their exoskeletons split open and they pull themselves out. The old exoskeleton is left behind. This process is called **molting**.

A female ornamental tarantula can be up to 2 inches (5 cm) long and have a leg span of more than 8 inches (20 cm)! Its fangs can grow nearly 1 inch (2.5 cm) long.

1 The ornamental tarantula makes its nest in a tree hollow. Unlike most tarantulas, ornamental **spiderlings** remain with their mother. She brings food to them — in this case, a large, green cricket.

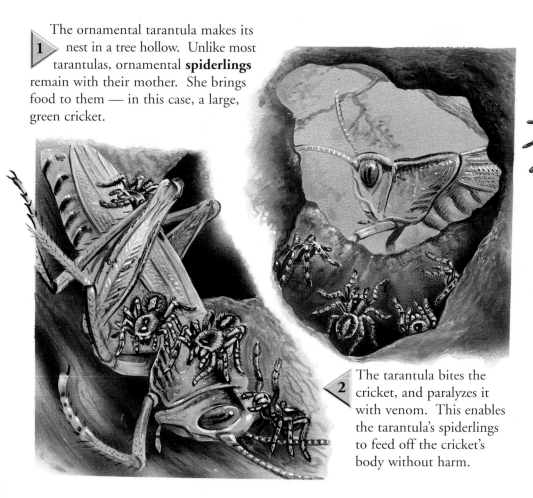

2 The tarantula bites the cricket, and paralyzes it with venom. This enables the tarantula's spiderlings to feed off the cricket's body without harm.

Where in the World

The ornamental tarantula lives in India. There are several kinds of ornamental tarantula.

Lynx Spider

The lynx spider has long skinny legs that allow it to jump more than twenty times its own length! The spider's legs are dotted with spines that help it locate prey.

The lynx spider has eight eyes, six of which are arranged in a hexagon pattern. It has excellent eyesight.

The lynx spider also senses its prey with the help of hairs on its pedipalps.

The lynx spider makes a strong web for catching small, flying insects. Special oily pads on the spider's feet allow it to walk around on the web without getting stuck.

The lynx spider is a jungle athlete. It launches itself into the air to catch its victims before they can escape.

1 The green lynx spider is well **camouflaged** against the plants. A bee comes to visit a flower and does not notice the spider lurking among the leaves.

2 The spider uses its vision to judge the distance to the bee. It then leaps upon the bee, sinking its fangs into the bee's body.

3 The spider injects venom into the bee that kills it in seconds, enabling the spider to feed.

Actual Size

Where in the World

This lynx spider lives in the United States, Mexico, and Central America.

Portia Spider

The Portia spider has unusually large eyes and excellent vision, which it uses to hunt.

The Portia spider has thick, bumpy legs that taper at the ends. The thin parts of the spider's legs enable it to move swiftly.

Long fangs at the front of the Portia spider's head can inject venom.

The spider is a creative killer that sneaks up on web-weaving spiders.

1 The Portia spider plans its approach carefully. Here it attracts an orb web spider, tapping its web like a trapped insect.

2 As the orb web spider approaches, the Portia spider suddenly launches an attack, burying its fangs in the orb spider's back!

Did You Know?

When stalking a hunting spider, the Portia watches its prey before attacking. It uses its sharp vision to approach its victim from a distance before pouncing! Such behavior is rare among spiders.

Where in the World

Portia spiders live in the **tropical** regions in Australia, Africa, and Asia.

Purse-Web Spider

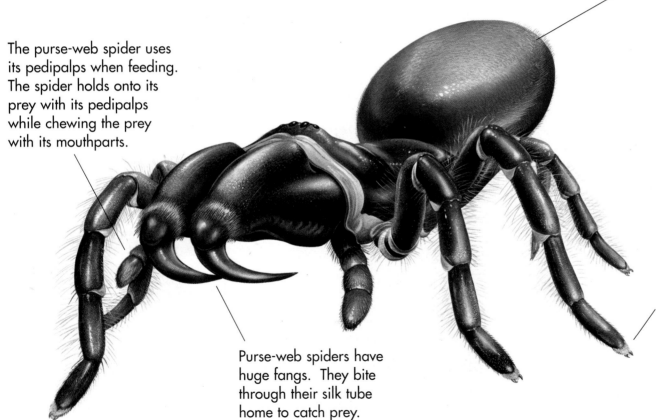

Female purse-web spiders have larger abdomens than males. Both male and female purse-web spiders have spinnerets.

The purse-web spider uses its pedipalps when feeding. The spider holds onto its prey with its pedipalps while chewing the prey with its mouthparts.

Purse-web spiders have short, thick legs. They cannot run fast. Their legs are perfectly **adapted** for moving around the small space inside silk tubes.

Purse-web spiders have huge fangs. They bite through their silk tube home to catch prey.

Purse-web spiders are nearly blind. They live underground, hidden inside silk-lined tubes. They use their sense of touch to feel the vibrations of prey moving above them.

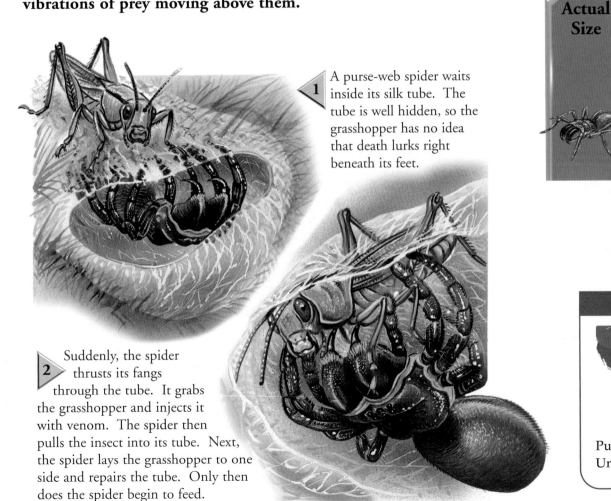

1 ▷ A purse-web spider waits inside its silk tube. The tube is well hidden, so the grasshopper has no idea that death lurks right beneath its feet.

2 ▷ Suddenly, the spider thrusts its fangs through the tube. It grabs the grasshopper and injects it with venom. The spider then pulls the insect into its tube. Next, the spider lays the grasshopper to one side and repairs the tube. Only then does the spider begin to feed.

Actual Size

Where in the World

Purse-web spiders live in the United States and Europe.

Baboon Spider

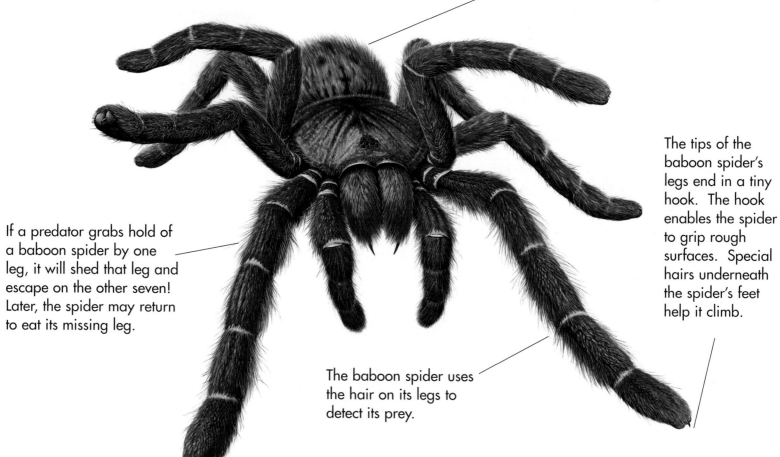

Like most tarantulas, the baboon spider is brown. This color helps it blend into the forest floor where it lives among dead leaves and twigs.

The tips of the baboon spider's legs end in a tiny hook. The hook enables the spider to grip rough surfaces. Special hairs underneath the spider's feet help it climb.

If a predator grabs hold of a baboon spider by one leg, it will shed that leg and escape on the other seven! Later, the spider may return to eat its missing leg.

The baboon spider uses the hair on its legs to detect its prey.

Baboon spiders were named for their long, hairy legs. Someone must have thought the spider's legs looked like the arms of a baboon, a type of African monkey!

1 Tarantulas make tasty meals for many large predators. This leopard cub has discovered a baboon spider on the forest floor. It tries to swat the spider with its paw.

2 Baboon spiders are aggressive. This spider quickly sinks its huge fangs into the leopard's paw. The cub then licks its injured paw and slinks off.

Spitting Spider

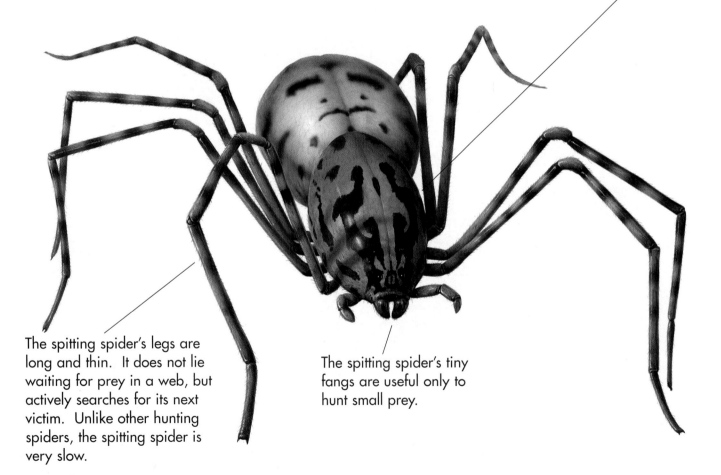

Silk is stored inside the spitting spider's unusually swollen head. The spider can actually spit silk through its mouth to catch prey!

The spitting spider's legs are long and thin. It does not lie waiting for prey in a web, but actively searches for its next victim. Unlike other hunting spiders, the spitting spider is very slow.

The spitting spider's tiny fangs are useful only to hunt small prey.

22

The spitting spider has six eyes and excellent vision. It needs good eyesight to aim its jet of poisonous, sticky silk at prey.

1 The spitting spider spots a fly. It slowly creeps forward until the fly is about 1 inch (2.5 cm) away. Then it strikes!

2 The spider spits sticky silk from its mouth at its prey. The fly is trapped. The spider can easily kill it with a poisonous bite.

Actual Size

Funnel-Web Spider

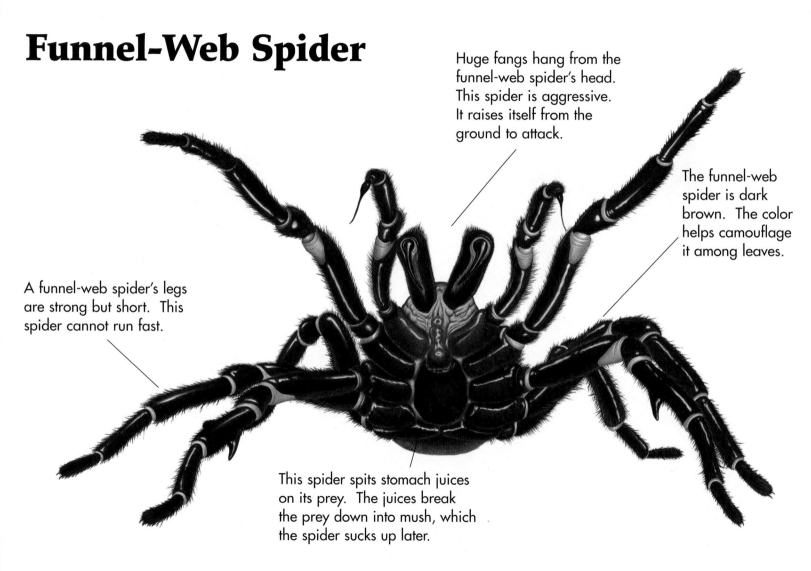

Huge fangs hang from the funnel-web spider's head. This spider is aggressive. It raises itself from the ground to attack.

The funnel-web spider is dark brown. The color helps camouflage it among leaves.

A funnel-web spider's legs are strong but short. This spider cannot run fast.

This spider spits stomach juices on its prey. The juices break the prey down into mush, which the spider sucks up later.

Funnel-web spiders use deadly venom. They killed at least thirteen people in Australia before **antivenin** was developed. Humans are usually bitten after a heavy rainfall. This is because rain often forces funnel-web spiders from their **burrows**.

1 The funnel-web spider makes a silk-lined burrow in the ground. Then it waits for prey. If an insect comes close, the spider rushes out and grabs it with its front legs. The spider kills the insect with a poisonous bite.

2 When the spider gets stressed, venom actually drips from its fangs!

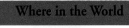

Size

Did You Know?

Scientists suspect that male funnel-web spiders are more venomous than females. In most kinds of spiders, females are more venomous than males. Scientists are still not sure why funnel-web spiders may be different.

Where in the World

The funnel-web spider lives along the eastern coast of Australia.

25

Trapdoor Spider

The trapdoor spider's legs are short and thick. They curve outward to make running in tunnels easier.

Trapdoor spiders have several tiny eyes, but poor eyesight. They instead use their sense of touch to catch prey.

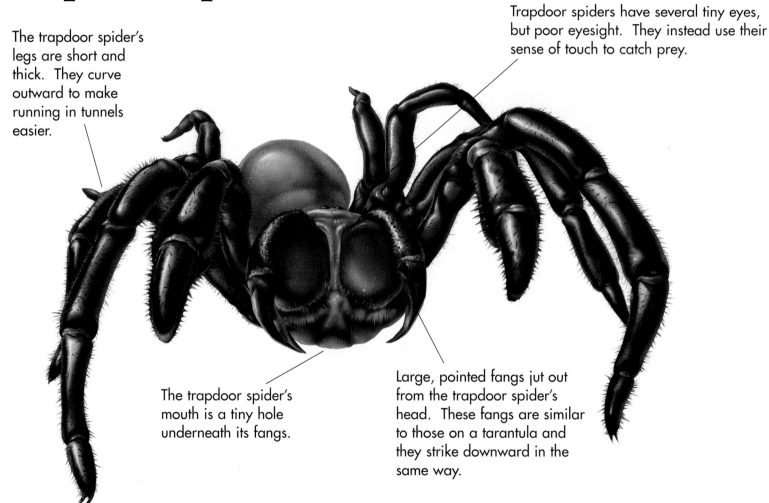

The trapdoor spider's mouth is a tiny hole underneath its fangs.

Large, pointed fangs jut out from the trapdoor spider's head. These fangs are similar to those on a tarantula and they strike downward in the same way.

The trapdoor spider surprises its prey from inside its silk-lined tunnel. Its home is capped with a hidden trapdoor. The trapdoor spider is a skilled digger with a quick reaction.

1 The trapdoor spider digs a tunnel into the ground. Then it lines the tunnel with silk. The spider also makes a lid of silk over the tunnel and covers it with dirt, leaves, and twigs.

2 The spider lays strands of silk along the ground. These strands end inside the tunnel. When an insect walks across the silk strands, the spider feels the movement inside its tunnel.

Actual Size

Did You Know?

Trapdoor spiders pounce on their prey with speed and accuracy. They protect their burrows from predators with separate lids and side tunnels for added safety.

3 The spider rushes out, grabs the insect, and pulls it back into the tunnel. The spider then kills the insect with a poisonous bite.

Where in the World

Trapdoor spiders live in most parts of the world, especially in the tropics.

Yellow Sac Spider

The yellow sac spider comes in many colors. They are often greenish yellow.

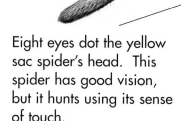

Eight eyes dot the yellow sac spider's head. This spider has good vision, but it hunts using its sense of touch.

The yellow sac spider has small fangs, but powerful venom.

Yellow sac spiders are **nocturnal**. They hide during the day and hunt at night. These spiders run quickly on their long, slender legs.

Yellow sac spiders are named after the flattened silk tubes where they live during the day. At night they chase down insects and inject them with venom.

Did You Know?

Most bites by yellow sac spiders are not serious. In some cases, the bite may cause surrounding **tissue** to die, leaving a nasty wound. Yellow sac spider bites have never killed anyone.

Where in the World

Yellow sac spiders live across much of the world.

Glossary

abdomen — the lower section of an insect's body

adapted — suited by nature to a particular use

aggressive — forceful, ready to attack

antivenin — a medication that stops a poison from being harmful

burrows — holes made in the ground by animals for shelter and protection

camouflaged — hidden or disguised by the pattern on an animal's skin

canopy — the uppermost layer of a forest

cocoons — sacs, pouches, or cases that help protect the larvae before they change into adults

exoskeleton — a tough skeleton on the outside of an animal's body

fangs — long teeth that often contain poison

injects — forces fluid or poison into a body

mating — joining together to produce babies

molting — the process of shedding an exoskeleton

mouthparts — the parts of an animal used for feeding

nocturnal — active at night

organs — parts of the body that do a specific job

paralyzed — a state of being unable to move

pedipalps — a pair of feelers between a spider's front legs

poisonous — having a deadly substance, such as venom, that causes illness or death

predator — animal that hunts, kills, and eats other animals for food

prey — an animal hunted and killed for food

silk glands — the parts of a spider's body that produce proteins to make silk for webbing

span — the distance between two points, such as the ends of opposite legs

spiderlings — baby spiders

spinnerets — the part of a spider's body that makes silk

tissue — a layer or mass of one kind of cell

toxic — poisonous

tropical — referring to the warmest regions of the world, with lush plant life and lots of rain

venom — a poison made by an animal

venomous — describing something containing poison

vibration — tiny motion caused by sound or movements

For More Information

Books

Dangerous Insects & Spiders. Nature's Monsters (series). Chris McNab (Gareth Stevens, 2006)

Spiders. Seymour Simon (HarperCollins, 2003)

Spiders. True Books (series). Ann O. Squire (Children's Press, 2004)

Spiders and Their Webs. Darlyne A. Murawski (National Geographic Children's Books, 2004)

Spiders Up Close. Minibeasts Up Close (series). Robin Birch (Raintree, 2004)

The Tarantula Scientist. Scientists in the Field (series). Sy Montgomery (Houghton Mifflin, 2007)

Web Sites

About Spiders — American Humane Association
www.americanhumane.org/kids/spiders.html

Giantspiders.com
giantspiders.com

Spider Identification – Venomous or Dangerous?
www.termite.com/spider-identification.html

Spider Myths
www.washington.edu/burkemuseum/spidermyth/index.html

Tarantulas.com
www.tarantulas.com

Publisher's note to educators and parents: Our editors have carefully reviewed these web sites to ensure that they are suitable for children. Many web sites change frequently, however, and we cannot guarantee that a site's future contents will continue to meet our high standards of quality and educational value. Be advised that children should be closely supervised whenever they access the Internet.

Index